AMAZING
JUNIOR
ATLAS
OF ANIMALS

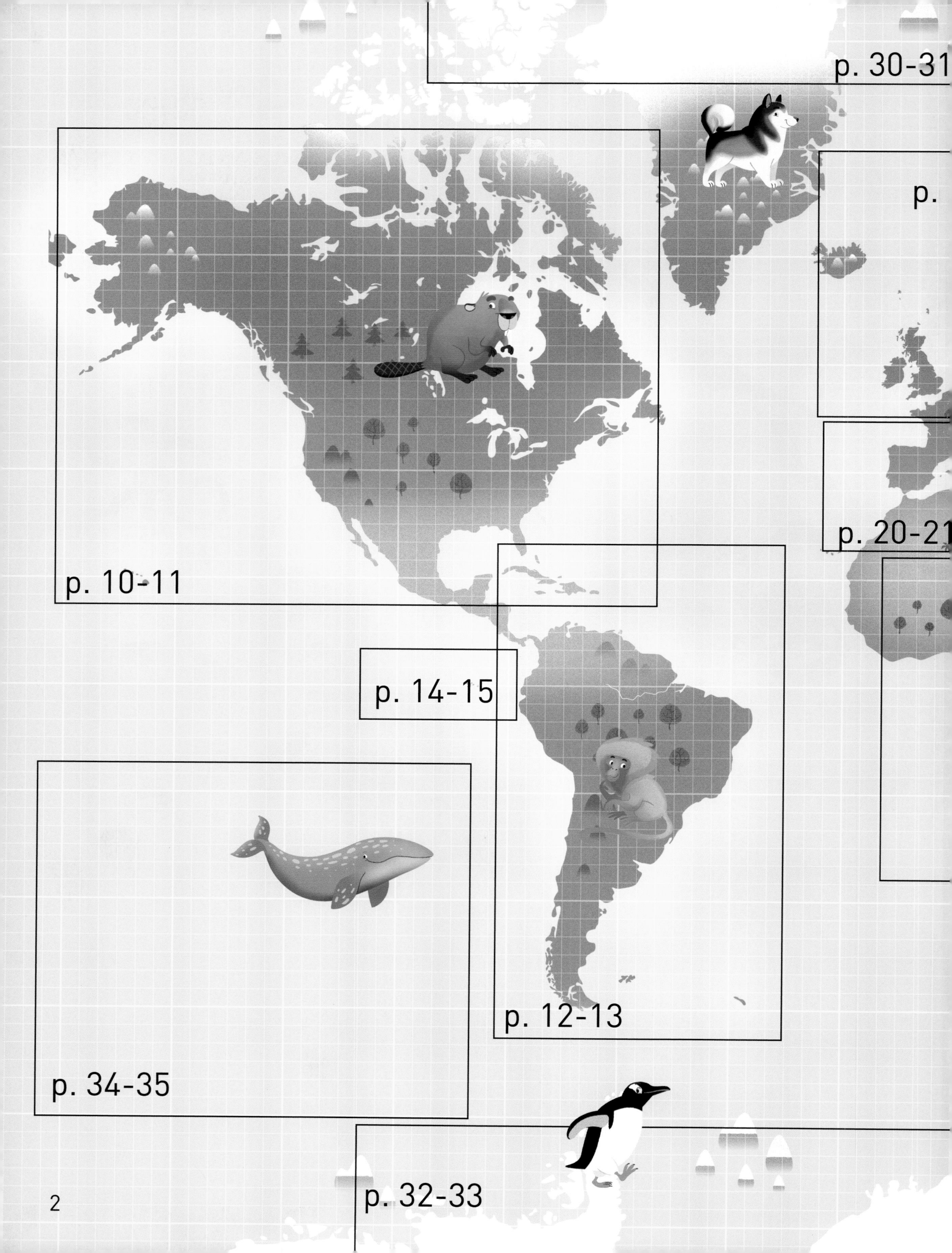
p. 30-31
p.
p. 10-11
p. 20-21
p. 14-15
p. 12-13
p. 34-35
p. 32-33

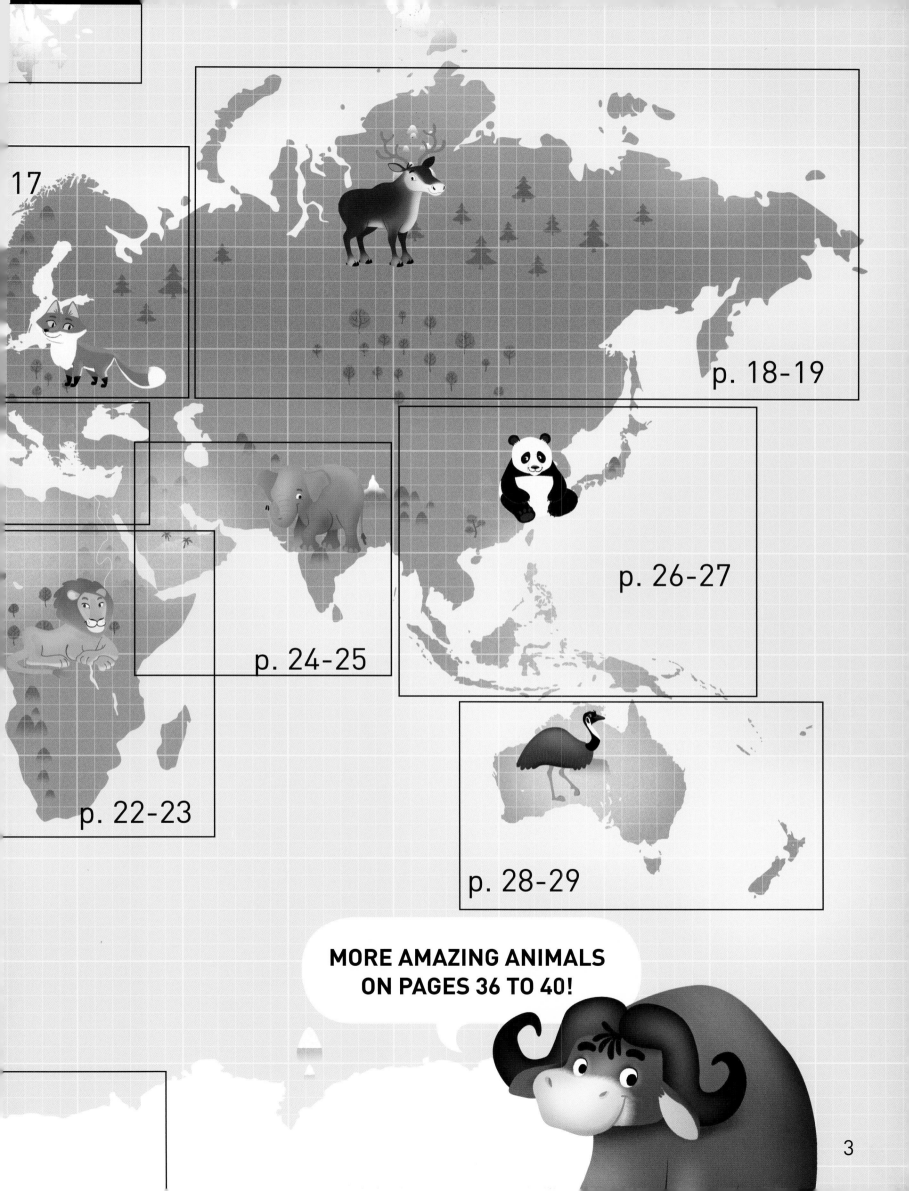

MORE AMAZING ANIMALS
ON PAGES 36 TO 40!

NORTH
AMERICA

North America forms a triangle with Alaska in the top left, Greenland in the top right and Panama at the bottom. Its climate is very diverse. In the southwest, it's hot, while the north can be icy cold. Besides deserts and snow, North America also has gorgeous grassy areas, superb swamps, magnificent mountains and fantastic forests. Such a diverse place is bound to be home to a wide range of animals.

Discover the animals of North America on pages 10 and 11.

SOUTH
AMERICA

Millions of years ago, before South America was connected to North America, it was more or less a giant island. As it had no contact with other parts of the world, plants and animal species developed that you won't find anywhere else. South America has the largest rainforest in the world as well as pampas, which are large grassland plains without any trees. Tropical coconut trees grow along the coastline. You'll find cold glaciers in the south. All these places house animals that are well adapted to their surroundings.

Discover the animals of South America on pages 12 and 13.

GALÁPAGOS
ISLANDS

Some of the world's most unique animals live off the South American coast, on islands born from volcanic eruptions. At first there was no life, but gradually more and more animals came to the islands. The ones that could not swim or fly reached the islands sitting on floating tree trunks or coconuts! All evolved in their own special ways to adapt to life on the islands.

Discover the animals of the Galápagos Islands on pages 14 and 15.

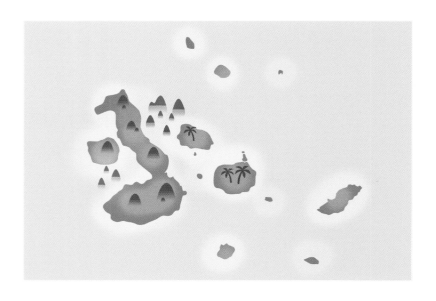

EUROPE

Europe is the second smallest continent. The Alps and Pyrenees mountains run straight through the middle, while the low-lying countries are partially below sea level! In the cool north, there are many forests and woodlands. In the warm south, it is much drier.
Since the landscape and climate vary across the continent, its animals live only in specific regions. Polar bears and Arctic foxes feel right at home in the cold, snowy north. The south has crickets, lizards and snakes that prefer a warmer and drier climate.

Discover the animals of Europe on pages 16 and 17.

EURASIA

Eurasia is the region where Europe and Asia meet. It mostly consists of Russia. It has cold winters and hot summers. In the north, the polar climate creates permanently frozen tundra, home to snow leopards, Siberian tigers and polar bears.

Discover the animals of Eurasia on pages 18 and 19.

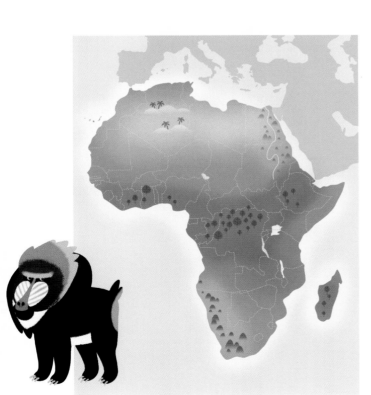

AFRICA

The second largest continent in the world lies to the south of Europe. Africa is known for its beautiful landscapes. The Sahara Desert covers much of the north, while tropical rainforests cover central Africa. It has a warm climate, but its mountains stay covered in snow most of the year.
Africa is home to many wild animals, including the 'Big Five', which are the elephant, rhino, leopard, lion and buffalo. They are called the big five because they are very big, very dangerous, and they have few natural enemies.

Discover the animals of Africa on pages 22 and 23.

NORTH **POLE**

When we talk about the North Pole, we usually refer to the Arctic area that includes the Arctic Ocean and parts of nearby continents. They are covered in ice for most of the year. Unlike Antarctica, which is a continent with land underneath the ice and snow, the Arctic is not a continent. The animals that live there are well adapted to the cold. It is the home of polar bears and Arctic foxes.

Discover the animals of the Arctic on pages 30 and 31.

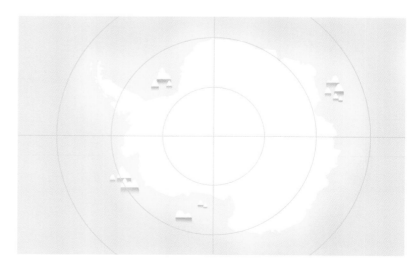

MIDDLE EAST **AND INDIA**

The Middle East, which is the southwest of Asia, is a hot, dry place. Even during the mild winters, little rain falls. It has deserts and steppes. But its animals are used to the environment. This region houses the world's lowest sea, the Dead Sea. Its water is extremely salty: not even fish can live in it.
India has a more diverse climate with a tropical south and a cold north with a variety of animals living in it.

Discover the animals of the Middle East on pages 24 and 25.

SOUTH **POLE**

Antarctica, or the South Pole, is the southern-most point of the world and it is the coldest place on Earth. This continent is actually a desert. The word 'desert' has nothing to do with sand. It just means that little rain falls in an area, and that is definitely true at Antarctica. The most famous inhabitants of this snow-covered region are the penguins.

Discover the animals of Antarctica on pages 32 and 33.

MEDITERRANEAN
SEA

The Mediterranean Sea and the nearby Black Sea form a region with mild winters and warm, dry summers. The north has a diverse animal population. The southern part is warm with desert areas and only animals that are accustomed to such a harsh environment live there.

Discover the animals of the Mediterranean area on pages 20 and 21.

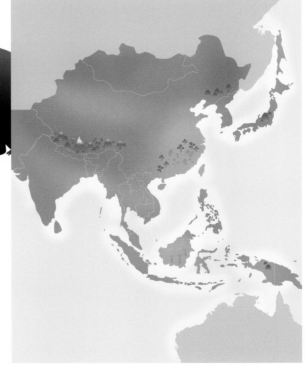

ASIA

Asia is the world's largest continent. Since it is so big, the climate varies from region to region. The northeast has hot and dry summers and freezing cold winters. Other parts are hot and humid and even have a rain season. It's also home to the world's highest mountain, Mount Everest.
The only wild pandas in the world live in the bamboo forests of China, while the rain forest of Indonesia is home to the world's only wild orangutans.

Discover the animals of Asia on pages 26 and 27.

OCEANIA

The smallest continent in the world is made up by many Pacific islands with a unique animal life. The climate varies: warm in the north, snow-covered mountains in the south, hot deserts in the west and rainforests in the east.
The Great Barrier Reef, just off the northeast coast of Australia, is rich with marine life. But this region is best known for its marsupials. These unique mammals, such as koalas and kangaroos, carry their young in pouches until they are old enough to care for themselves.

Discover the animals of Oceania on pages 28 and 29.

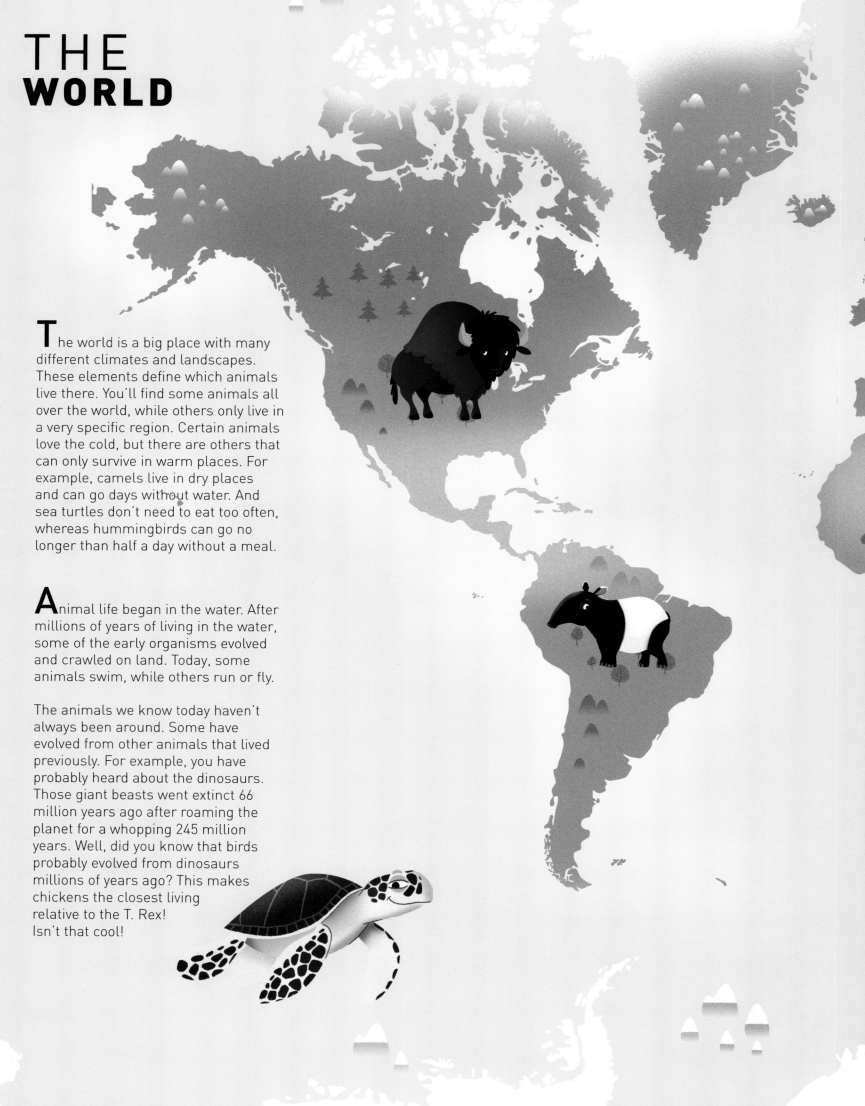

THE
WORLD

The world is a big place with many different climates and landscapes. These elements define which animals live there. You'll find some animals all over the world, while others only live in a very specific region. Certain animals love the cold, but there are others that can only survive in warm places. For example, camels live in dry places and can go days without water. And sea turtles don't need to eat too often, whereas hummingbirds can go no longer than half a day without a meal.

Animal life began in the water. After millions of years of living in the water, some of the early organisms evolved and crawled on land. Today, some animals swim, while others run or fly.

The animals we know today haven't always been around. Some have evolved from other animals that lived previously. For example, you have probably heard about the dinosaurs. Those giant beasts went extinct 66 million years ago after roaming the planet for a whopping 245 million years. Well, did you know that birds probably evolved from dinosaurs millions of years ago? This makes chickens the closest living relative to the T. Rex! Isn't that cool!

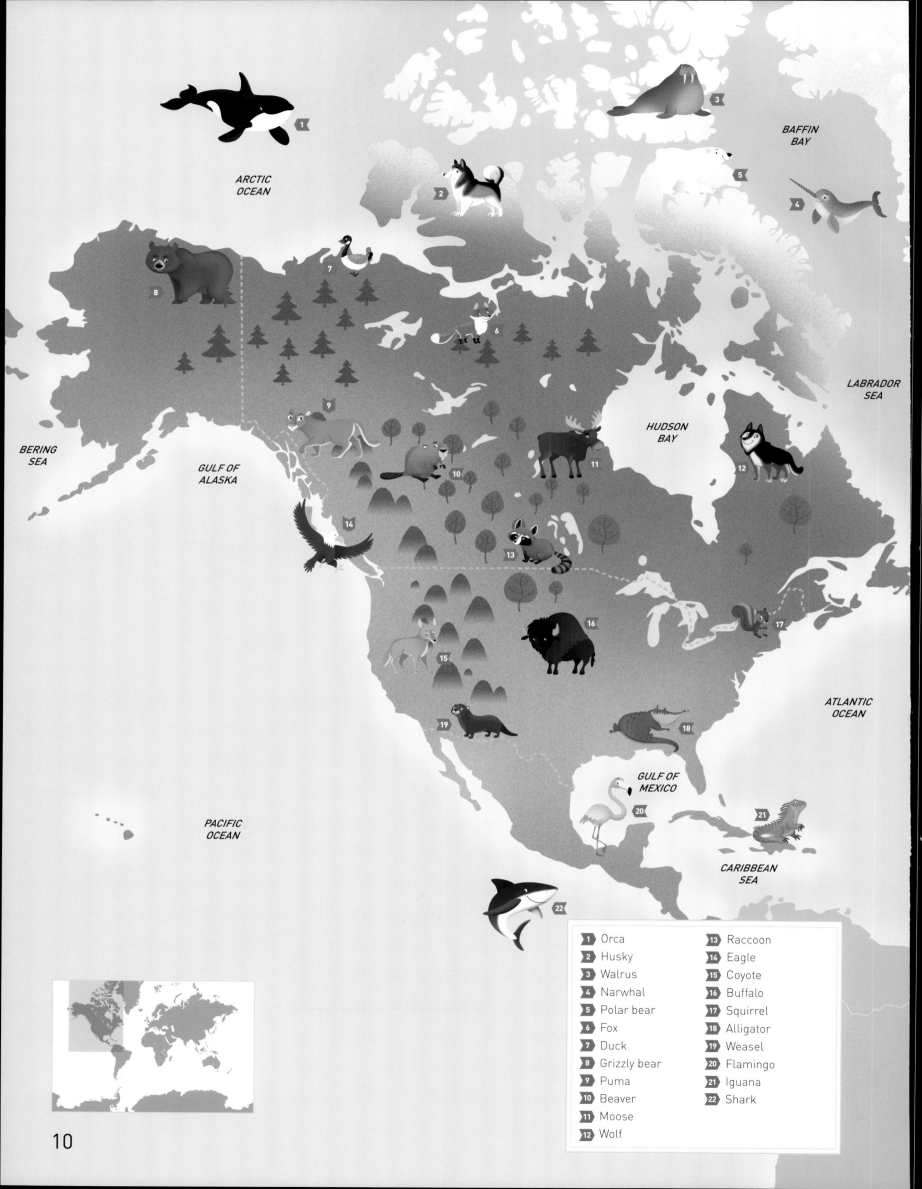

ARCTIC
OCEAN

BAFFIN
BAY

LABRADOR
SEA

BERING
SEA

GULF OF
ALASKA

HUDSON
BAY

ATLANTIC
OCEAN

PACIFIC
OCEAN

GULF OF
MEXICO

CARIBBEAN
SEA

1	Orca	13	Raccoon
2	Husky	14	Eagle
3	Walrus	15	Coyote
4	Narwhal	16	Buffalo
5	Polar bear	17	Squirrel
6	Fox	18	Alligator
7	Duck	19	Weasel
8	Grizzly bear	20	Flamingo
9	Puma	21	Iguana
10	Beaver	22	Shark
11	Moose		
12	Wolf		

NORTH AMERICA

Grizzly bear
This large bear is found in wooded areas and can be recognised by the large, muscular hump on its neck. Its coat is black, brown or blond. It mostly eats grass, berries, and fish. During winter, it hibernates in a mountain cave for months at a time.

Eagle
Its wings are each a metre long, so it's no wonder this predator flies like the wind! It can glide in the air for hours at a time, hunting for the perfect bite. It has excellent eyesight to help spot the small animals, such as rabbits, birds and fish, that make up its diet.

Alligator
These cold-blooded reptiles have been on Earth for millions of years. The gender of their young is determined by the temperature of their eggs: warmer eggs hatch into boys, colder ones into girls.

Raccoon
About the size of a fox, this clever creature has a thick, grey tail with black rings. The black mask covering its eyes makes it look like a masked bandit! It prefers to live in wooded areas close to water. But with fewer forests around, a raccoon will move to towns to scavenge food from our garbage.

Raccoons laze around during the day in a quiet place, but when darkness begins to fall, they go in search of food. Eating plants, fruits, eggs, insects, snails and even frogs, this predator is by no means a picky eater!

Puma
This agile creature is often called a 'mountain lion'. It is quite shy and prefers to live in places uninhabited by people. These big cats usually hunt in the morning or evening. Real meat-eaters, their favourite dish is deer.

Among the fastest cats in the world, the puma has a long, thick tail and sturdy legs. Its back legs are longer than its front legs, making the puma an excellent jumper. To give you an idea of its amazing jumping abilities: starting on the ground, a puma could leap over a garage or shed with ease. With a run-up, it can jump as high as the second floor of a house. Not many animals can do this!

SOUTH AMERICA

Toucan
This bird is famous for its big, colourful beak. Among the 40 different species of toucan, many have a yellow, orange, red or green beak. There are even toucans whose beaks include all the colours of the rainbow.

Anteater
You guessed it, this creature eats ants and lots of them: up to 30,000 a day! It sneaks its enormous and toothless snout into an ant nest, and quickly flicks its tongue in and out of its mouth, sucking all the ants out of their nest.
To fill its tummy, it visits up to 200 nests a day!

Sloth
Spending most of their life in trees, these sloths nap up to 15 hours a day! When awake, they hardly move so they don't need a lot of food for energy. They have fruits, leaves and twigs on their menu, nothing that they can't find in their own trees.

A sloth will only leave its tree about once a week to go to the toilet on the ground. Because sloths are usually just hanging from a tree branch, the hair on their bellies parts to the sides. Handy, because this helps the rainwater flow down, and in the rainforest, there is a lot of rain.

Grapsus grapsus
With its five pairs of legs, this crab, who's also known as 'red rock crab' or 'Sally Lightfoot', is fast, agile, and hard to catch. Its colour varies from brownish-red to pink, yellow, and orange.

Living on rocky beaches, it can withstand strong waves by holding on tightly to the rocks. It mostly eats algae, but given half a chance, it will gladly add sea creatures like mussels or snails to its menu. It's also know as a cleaner, eating dead fish and sometimes even the ticks of marine iguanas.

Flamingo
This bird loves warm, watery places. It's a strong flyer and a good swimmer, but it spends most of its time wading in the water or standing on one leg.

Living in enormous colonies of up to a thousand birds, the brightly coloured flamingo finds safety in numbers.
Its pink feathers are the result of its diet. When ill, a flamingo will turn pale.

1	Flamingo	11	Tapir
2	Shark	12	Anteater
3	Iguana	13	Llama
4	Sea turtle	14	Golden lion tamarin
5	Guinea pig	15	Toucan
6	Parrot	16	Chameleon
7	Capuchin monkey	17	Sailfish
8	Grapsus grapsus	18	Orca
9	Common marmoset	19	Gentoo penguin
10	Sloth		

GULF OF MEXICO

CARIBBEAN SEA

NORTH ATLANTIC OCEAN

PACIFIC OCEAN

SOUTH ATLANTIC OCEAN

GALÁPAGOS
ISLANDS

Darwin

In 1831 a ship called 'Beagle' went on an expedition with scientist Charles Darwin on board. By researching the animals on the Galápagos Islands he discovered that animals must evolve.

The Galápagos animals are truly unique. They aren't found anywhere else in the world. The islands' most famous inhabitant is the giant tortoise. The islands are even named after it: the word 'galápago' is Spanish for 'tortoise'. Visitors are amazed to find that most animals are not afraid of them. Since there are no large land predators or venomous snakes, the animals living there are mostly tame, because they've never had to defend themselves against enemies.

Marine Leguana

Unique among its kind, this is the only iguana in the world that can swim. It forages for food in the water, with algae being the only dish on its menu. After swimming and eating, it takes a much needed rest on the rocks, sunbathing to warm up its body.

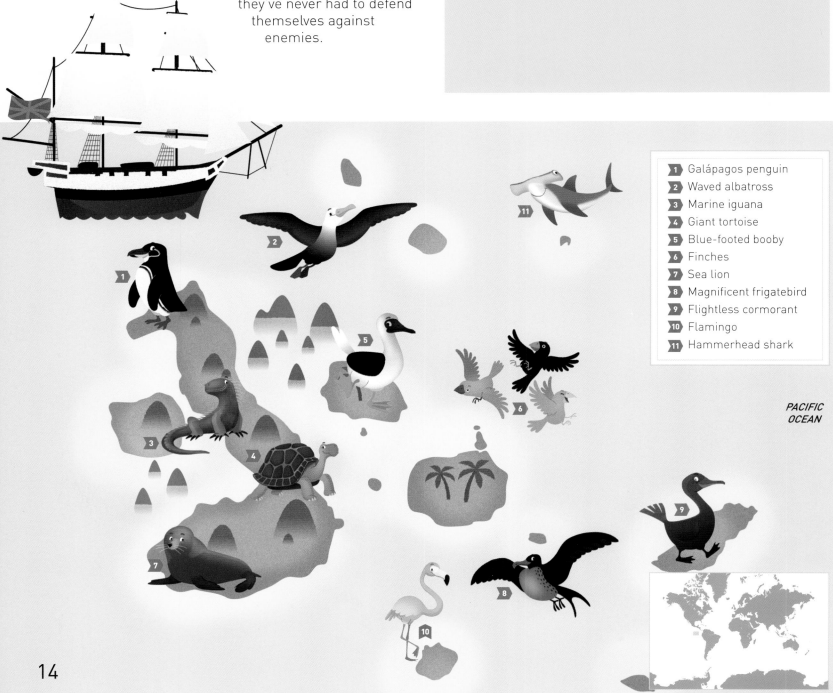

1. Galápagos penguin
2. Waved albatross
3. Marine iguana
4. Giant tortoise
5. Blue-footed booby
6. Finches
7. Sea lion
8. Magnificent frigatebird
9. Flightless cormorant
10. Flamingo
11. Hammerhead shark

PACIFIC OCEAN

FLIGHTLESS CORMORANT

This bird is the largest of its kind but also the only cormorant in the world that can't fly. It hunts for fish by diving into the water. Unfortunately its feathers aren't waterproof, making it necessary to sun-dry its wings after each dive.

Long ago, the ancestors of these birds were good flyers. But after years and years without enemies on the islands, their bodies eventually evolved, making them flightless.

WAVED ALBATROSS

Also known as the Galápagos albatross, this is the largest bird on the islands. It has a wingspan of 2.5 metres.

MAGNIFICENT FRIGATEBIRD

This bird has black feathers with a white bill for the females and a bright red bill for the males. The magnificent frigatebird is the largest of its species. Its very large wingspan makes it an excellent flyer and glider. Not surprisingly, it spends most of its time in the air, looking for food.

Research has shown that the frigatebirds on the Galápagos Islands haven't mated with other frigatebirds for hundreds of thousands of years!

SEA LION

On the Galápagos Islands, you don't have to look long to spot a sun-bathing or playful sea lion. They are everywhere.
They mostly feed on sardines, but due to climate changes there are fewer sardines in the region. This is one of the reasons why this breed of sea lions is now considered endangered.

BLUE-FOOTED BOOBY

'The bluer the better' is this bird's motto. The males will proudly show off their bright blue feet, hoping to impress the ladies. During the day, they soar the skies, flying far out to sea, keeping an eye open for fish. Besides being good flyers, boobies are also skilled divers.
It is said that the name 'booby' comes from the Spanish word 'bobo', meaning 'silly', because the first people to encounter this bird thought they looked funny, walking on their blue feet.

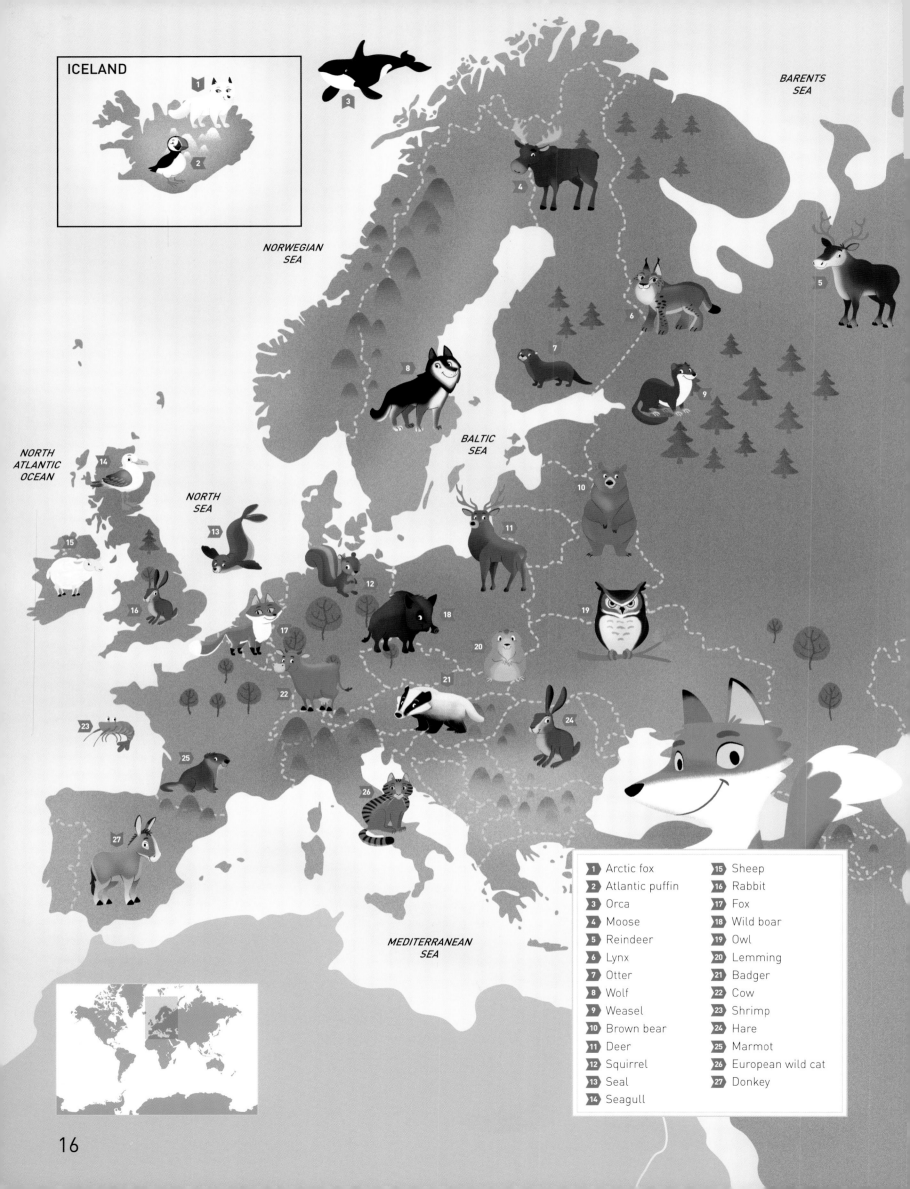

ICELAND

NORWEGIAN
SEA

BARENTS
SEA

NORTH
ATLANTIC
OCEAN

NORTH
SEA

BALTIC
SEA

MEDITERRANEAN
SEA

1	Arctic fox	15	Sheep
2	Atlantic puffin	16	Rabbit
3	Orca	17	Fox
4	Moose	18	Wild boar
5	Reindeer	19	Owl
6	Lynx	20	Lemming
7	Otter	21	Badger
8	Wolf	22	Cow
9	Weasel	23	Shrimp
10	Brown bear	24	Hare
11	Deer	25	Marmot
12	Squirrel	26	European wild cat
13	Seal	27	Donkey
14	Seagull		

EUROPE

Owl

Almost all owls are nocturnal. This means that they are most active at night. They sit upright on the lookout, keeping a keen eye out for a yummy snack like a mouse or a small bird.

An owl is easily recognised by its flat face and sharp beak. Since its eyes can't move on their own, it has to turn its head to look around. Luckily its flexible neck allows it to turn a whopping 270 degrees.

Jay

The jay will screech at the sight of danger, but its real talent is mimicry. It can imitate the sound of different types of birds in order to mislead both its enemies and its prey.

Weasel

This small mammal has a slender body, a long neck and short legs. Its coat is mostly reddish or brown with white fur on its belly. In the winter months, some weasels might grow a completely white fur coat to match their snowy surroundings.

Don't let its size mislead you; this small predator is a skilled hunter, killing its prey with a single bite to the neck. Even if it isn't hungry, a weasel will still hunt, storing its leftover catch in cold dens as an extra wintertime snack.

Red fox

With its red fur, bushy tail, and dog-like appearance, the fox might look like a nice pet, but this wild animal prefers to live alone.

The fox most often lives in an underground burrow. It is an intelligent predator and sees very well in the dark, allowing it to hunt both day and night.

Hedgehog

The cute-looking hedgehog has a spiky defence to scare off enemies. When in danger, it rolls itself up into a small, prickly ball. Enemies think twice before biting it and leave it well alone!

Mole

With its very strong forelimbs and large paws, a mole can easily dig long underground tunnels. The tunnel structure is designed to help him catch his favourite meal: earthworms.

Deer

Elk, moose, reindeer, chital, etc.: there are many types of deer. What all the European varieties have in common is that each year the male deer will grow and shed new antlers after the mating season.

Two deer will butt antlers, hoping to impress a mate. While they do this, the antlers will stop the deer from hurting their face and eyes.

EURASIA

BROWN BEAR

The brown bear's fur can range from light brown to almost black. It has a round head and can weigh up to 350 kilograms! It usually lives alone, except when it has cubs to care for. Female brown bears can actually give birth during their hibernation period.

BADGER

This nocturnal predator has black and white stripes on its head, a chubby body and short legs for digging. It has diverse meals with plants, fruits, insects and mice on the menu.
It lives with its family at the edge of the woods, in a large underground den. This den or sett has many rooms and tunnels with more than one way in and out. Handy when the den is under attack.

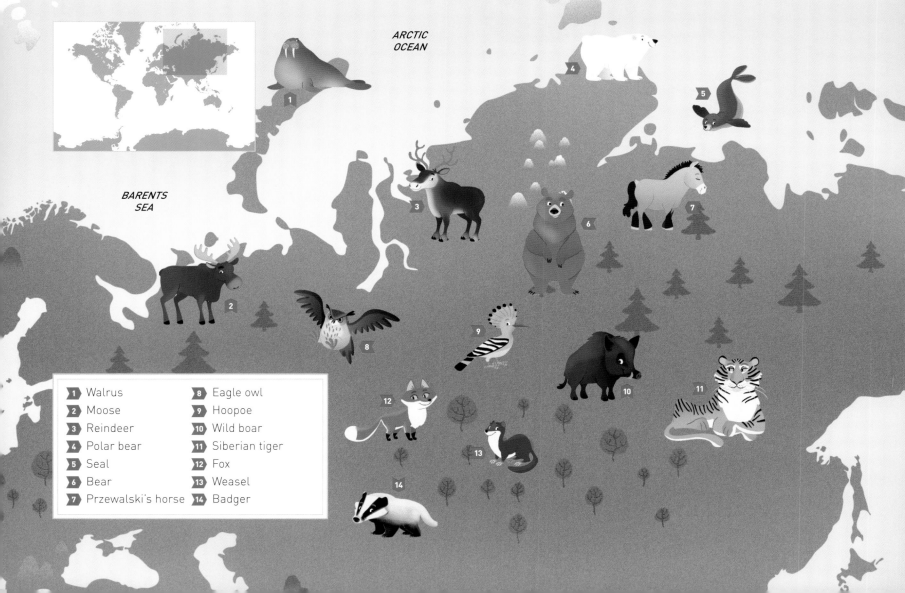

ARCTIC OCEAN

BARENTS SEA

1	Walrus	8	Eagle owl
2	Moose	9	Hoopoe
3	Reindeer	10	Wild boar
4	Polar bear	11	Siberian tiger
5	Seal	12	Fox
6	Bear	13	Weasel
7	Przewalski's horse	14	Badger

European Eagle Owl

The European eagle owl is the world's largest owl. It can grow to be about 75 centimetres tall with a wingspan of 188 centimetres.
This winged predator can be recognised by its flamboyant ear tufts and orange-coloured eyes.

Przewalski's Horse

You can't ride a Przewalski's horse: they are untameable! Unlike the tame horses you may have seen in stables and meadows, wild horses have never been domesticated.

The Przewalski's horse is the only breed of horse that is still truly wild. It can only be found Mongolia. Unfortunately, they are endangered and all of them now live in captivity.

Reindeer

Living in colder regions, this big deer has woolly fur and amongst the largest antlers of all deer. All adults, both male and female, grow a new set of antlers yearly.

Reindeer will feed on moss, grass and the leaves of willows and birches. Some might even add small rodents or fish to their diet.

Siberian Tiger

The largest wild cats alive are the Siberian tigers. They live in cold and harsh climates, preferring woodlands. Each Siberian tiger has a unique set of stripes. Living alone, it uses its scent to scare away other enemies. Cubs, however, will live with their mothers until they are two to three years old.

This tiger is endangered and risks extinction due to loss of woodlands and being hunted by people as trophies. It is estimated that less than 500 of these tigers still live in the wild.

MEDITERRANEAN SEA
SOUTH EUROPE AND NORTH AFRICA

Dromedary and Camel

In the desert, days can be extremely hot and nights extremely cold. Luckily, camels and dromedaries are adapted to these harsh conditions. Most camels have two humps on their back, the dromedary, however, is a camel with only one hump.

These humps contain fat. When the camel can't find enough to eat, it gets its energy from the fat stored in its humps. Camels can also survive for weeks without water. When they finally find water, they immediately drink massive amounts of it and store it in their fat.

Fennec fox

The smallest of the dog family calls the Sahara Desert of North Africa home. It lives with its family in underground dens.

Well adapted to life in the desert, this fox doesn't drink much water. Its fur is light coloured to keep it cool during the hot day, and fluffy to keep it warm during the night. Furry soles protect its feet from the hot sand. Its big ears help it to hear prey, with the added bonus that they cool down the fox.

Ibex

This wild goat is a good climber, so it is quite common in mountainous regions. The ibex is easily recognised by the two giant horns on its head that often curl towards the back.
The same as a cow, the ibex has four chambers in its stomach to help digest food.

Hoopoe

Slightly smaller than a common pigeon, this bird is found in Africa, Europe and Asia. In many languages its name refers to the 'oop-oop' sound it makes.
It has pinkish brown or chestnut coloured feathers, but its most notable characteristics are its crown of feathers, its long, sharp beak and its black-and-white-striped wings and tail.

Fun fact: to win a female's love, the male hoopoe will feed her insects.

Donkey

This relative of the horse has long ears and a tassel at the end of its tail. Preferring the company of others, it lives in herds, spending most of its time grazing.

Originating from dry desert areas, the donkey's fur is suited to hot and cold weather, but its coat isn't waterproof, so it does not like the rain.

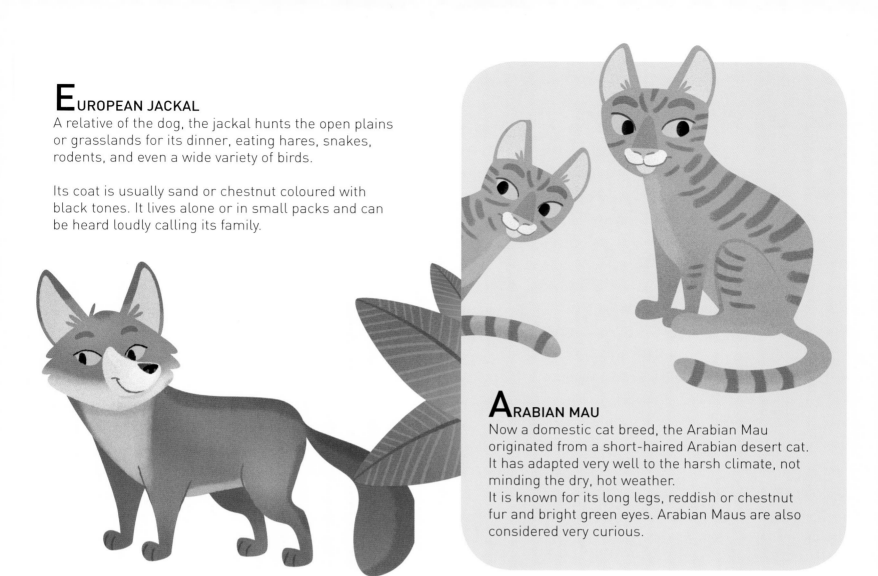

European jackal

A relative of the dog, the jackal hunts the open plains or grasslands for its dinner, eating hares, snakes, rodents, and even a wide variety of birds.

Its coat is usually sand or chestnut coloured with black tones. It lives alone or in small packs and can be heard loudly calling its family.

Arabian Mau

Now a domestic cat breed, the Arabian Mau originated from a short-haired Arabian desert cat. It has adapted very well to the harsh climate, not minding the dry, hot weather.
It is known for its long legs, reddish or chestnut fur and bright green eyes. Arabian Maus are also considered very curious.

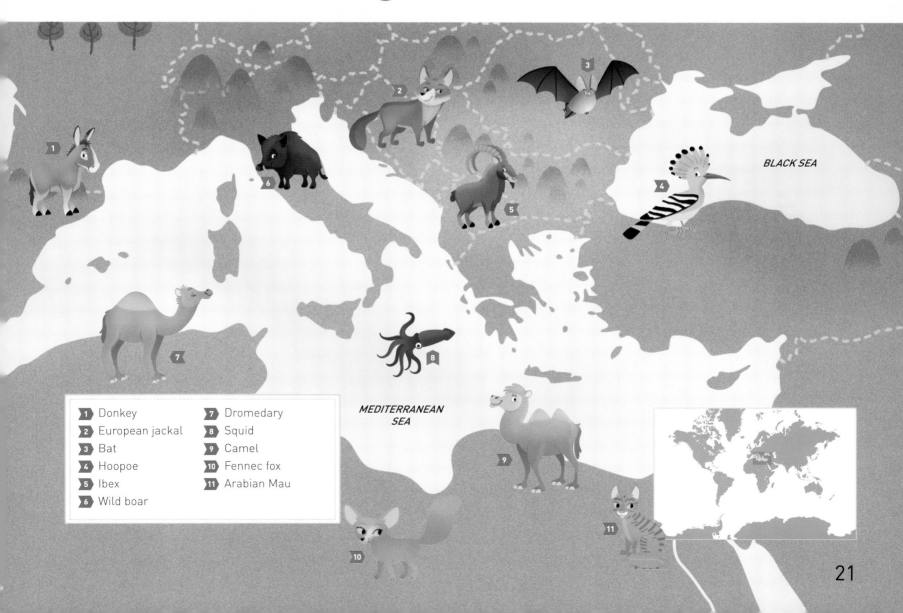

BLACK SEA

MEDITERRANEAN SEA

1 Donkey
2 European jackal
3 Bat
4 Hoopoe
5 Ibex
6 Wild boar
7 Dromedary
8 Squid
9 Camel
10 Fennec fox
11 Arabian Mau

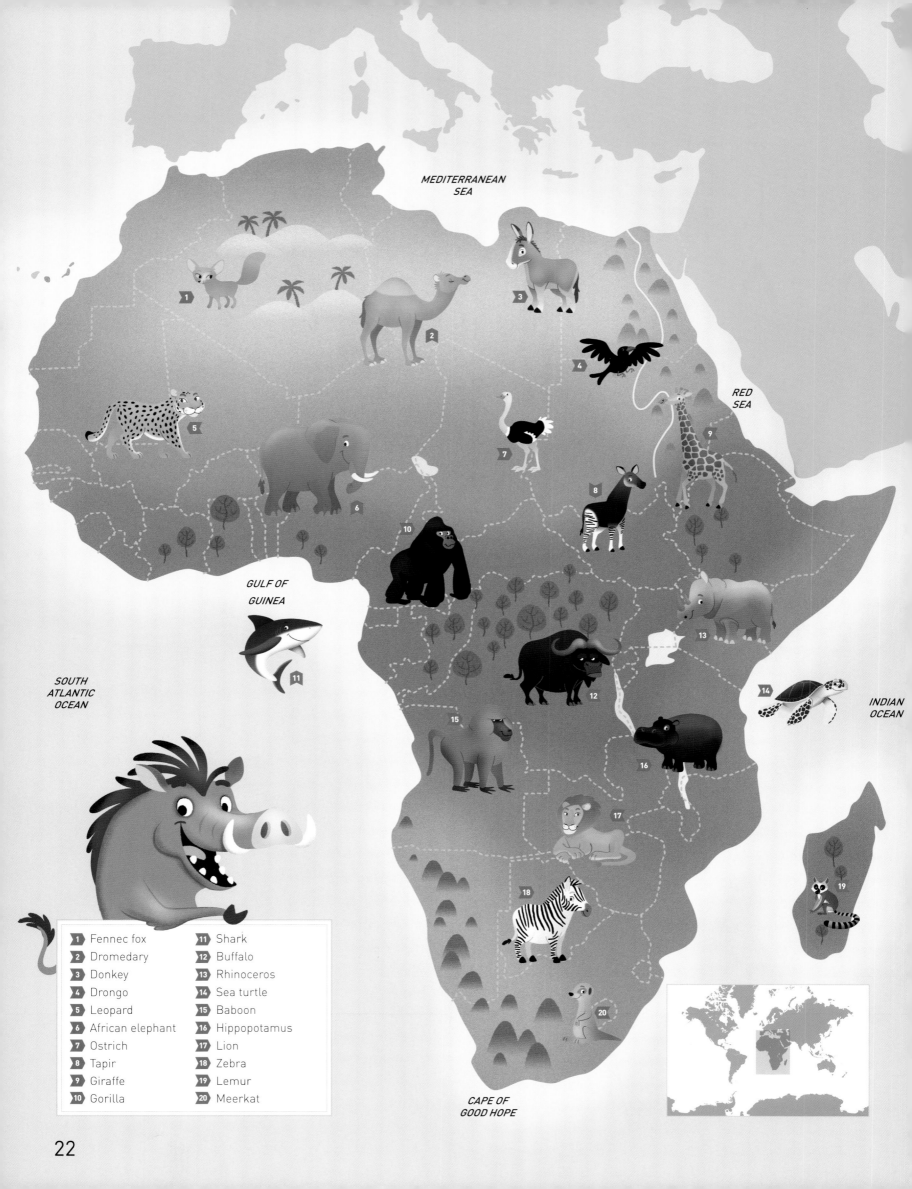

MEDITERRANEAN
SEA

RED
SEA

GULF OF
GUINEA

SOUTH
ATLANTIC
OCEAN

INDIAN
OCEAN

CAPE OF
GOOD HOPE

1	Fennec fox	11	Shark
2	Dromedary	12	Buffalo
3	Donkey	13	Rhinoceros
4	Drongo	14	Sea turtle
5	Leopard	15	Baboon
6	African elephant	16	Hippopotamus
7	Ostrich	17	Lion
8	Tapir	18	Zebra
9	Giraffe	19	Lemur
10	Gorilla	20	Meerkat

AFRICA

Gorilla

Primates are apes that have many similarities to people. They can walk on two legs, they have arms and hands, and they don't have a tail. The largest primate is the gorilla. It feels most at home in tropical rainforests, where it lives with its family.

Lion

Male lions look impressive with their big manes. On the grassy plains, this cat is king. Lionesses hunt together during the morning, before it gets too hot, and spend the rest of the day lazing in the shadows of trees. Their young cubs play fight with each other, which helps them to learn how to hunt.

Ostrich

Africa is home to the largest and heaviest bird in the world, the ostrich. Even its eggs are enormous. 24 chicken eggs could easily fit inside a single ostrich egg. Ostriches can't fly, but they can run extremely fast, making them the fastest running bird in the world. They can also give a powerful kick!

Ostriches don't have teeth to chew their food, so they eat stones to help grind their food down in their stomachs. An adult ostrich has about one kilo of stones in its stomach.

Giraffe

With its long neck and legs, giraffes are the tallest of all the land animals. They love the juicy leaves of trees. Instead of biting them off with their teeth, they pull them off with their black tongues, which are almost half a metre long!

Baby giraffes have an adventurous start to life. Their mother gives birth standing up, so the baby falls two metres to the ground! Thanks to its strong legs, the baby can stand and walk almost immediately.

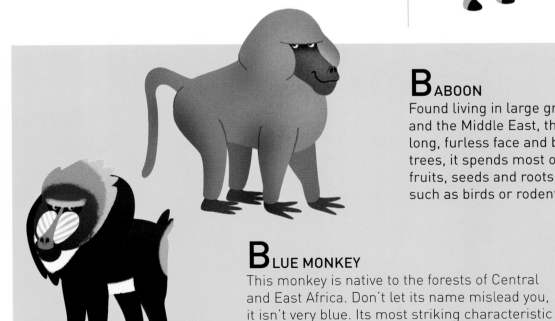

Baboon

Found living in large groups in the savannahs of Africa and the Middle East, the baboon is easily recognised by its long, furless face and bare bottom. Although it can climb trees, it spends most of its time on the ground. It will eat fruits, seeds and roots, but won't turn down a meaty dish such as birds or rodents.

Blue Monkey

This monkey is native to the forests of Central and East Africa. Don't let its name mislead you, it isn't very blue. Its most striking characteristic is its long tail.

MIDDLE EAST
AND INDIA

Asian ELEPHANT

The elephant, a grey animal with big ears and a long trunk, is the largest land animal on Earth. Its trunk is used to smell, drink, squirt water and even grab things.

Distinguishing Asian elephants from their African family can be difficult. Luckily, there are some distinct differences. The Asian elephant, found in the Asian tropical forests, is smaller than its African counterpart and it has significantly smaller, rounder ears. Also, all African elephants, male and female, have tusks, whereas most Asian elephants don't. The Asian elephant can also be recognised by the two humps on the top of its head.

Grey LANGUR

Although it prefers rainforests in India, you'll find this monkey in arid deserts, mangroves, mountains and forests. It easily adapts to its surroundings.

This large, slender monkey is grey with a black face and black ears. Spending as much time on the ground as in trees, it will often curl up its long tail when walking.

Ibis

Depending on the type, this big bird can have black, brown or white feathers. It has a long curved beak that makes it easy to search for food. For dinner, it will eat both plants and animals, favouring fish and crabs.

Ibis live together in flocks. They prefer to be near water and are often found wading in wetlands. However, they will nest up high in trees.

Peafowl

The male peafowl, or peacock, has a crown and an impressive tail with colourful feathers. He will fan out his tail to impress the peahens. In the mornings and evenings, this bird will search the ground for seeds, berries and insects to eat. When it's time to rest, it will find a nice branch in a tree to sleep.

Goat

The domesticated goats, known from farms and petting zoos, originate from the wild goats of Asia and Europe. The goat was domesticated nearly 10,000 years ago. It has a curious and intelligent nature and is known as a good climber with an excellent sense of balance.

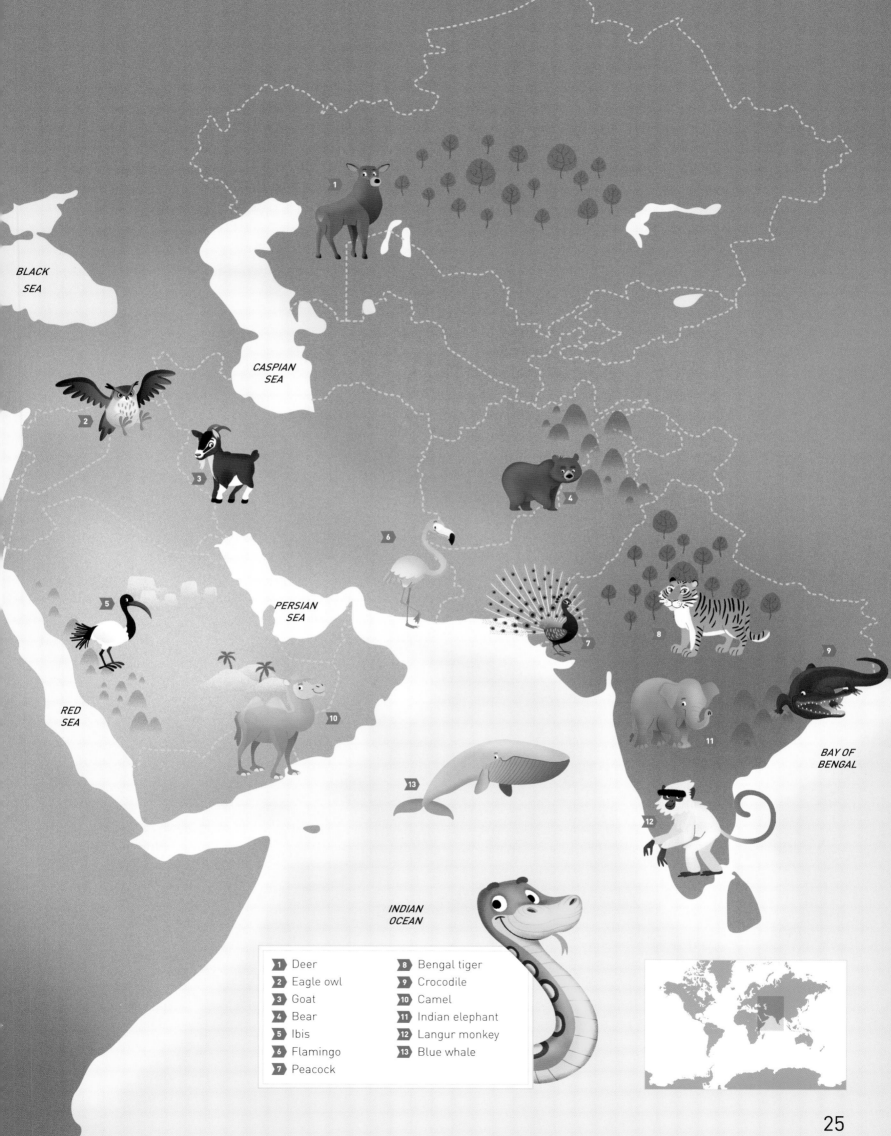

BLACK
SEA

CASPIAN
SEA

PERSIAN
SEA

RED
SEA

INDIAN
OCEAN

BAY OF
BENGAL

1	Deer	8	Bengal tiger
2	Eagle owl	9	Crocodile
3	Goat	10	Camel
4	Bear	11	Indian elephant
5	Ibis	12	Langur monkey
6	Flamingo	13	Blue whale
7	Peacock		

EAST
CHINA SEA

PACIFIC
OCEAN

PHILIPPINE
SEA

SOUTH
CHINA SEA

BAY OF
BENGAL

INDIAN
OCEAN

1	Reindeer	**8**	Bengal tiger
2	Lynx	**9**	Octopus
3	Przewalski's horse	**10**	Orangutan
4	Red panda	**11**	Proboscis monkey
5	Giant panda	**12**	Sea turtle
6	Cormorant	**13**	Hammerhead shark
7	Snow monkey		

ASIA
CHINA, JAPAN, MONGOLIA

Red Panda

Bamboo forests are home to the giant panda and the red panda. Both love to munch on bamboo, but they are not related. The small red panda has sharp claws, making it an excellent climber.

Its furry coat is so thick that it can overheat on sunny days. As such, the red panda will sleep most of the day high up in a tree, using its long, fluffy tail as a nice, soft blanket or cushion!

Orangutan

The orangutan is one of Asia's many apes. In Indonesia, the word orangutan means 'person of the forest'. With its long arms and strong hands and feet, this primate can easily climb trees.

High up in the treetops, this ape finds everything it needs: yummy leaves and fruit to eat and plenty of rainwater to drink. Orangutans also sleep in the trees, building a new nest every night out of branches and leaves.

Proboscis Monkey

The proboscis monkey is also known as the 'long-nosed monkey', so it comes as no surprise that it can easily be recognised by its very long nose. It is thought that their giant noses help them to make loud sounds to attract mates.

This monkey lives in Borneo, always staying near water. They are the best swimmers of all monkeys.

Cormorant

This fish-eating bird is an excellent diver, using its feet and wings to swim. Due to this, in the past, it has been trained to fish for humans in Japan and China. It would catch fish with its beak, but wouldn't swallow them. Instead it would deliver the fish to the fishermen's boat.

Giant Panda

The giant panda is easily recognised by its white head, black ears and black patches around its eyes. 'Panda' is Nepalese for 'bamboo-eater'; it eats several kilos of bamboo every day. It even has an extra thumb on its front paws to help it grip bamboo sticks firmly.

Pandas like to be left alone, so they brush their short tails against their bamboo stalks, marking them with their scent. This lets other pandas know when they are in another panda's territory. Unfortunately, the bamboo forests are shrinking, endangering the panda species.

OCEANIA

Platypus

Maybe one of the oddest looking animals in the world, the platypus has the beak of a duck, the body of an otter and the tail of a beaver. If that isn't unique enough it also has poisonous spikes on its ankles. And even though it's a mammal... it lays eggs.

The platypus lives in rivers, where it sleeps during the day in a self-dug burrow. At night, it uses its beak to root around in the mud for food. Worms, frogs, freshwater shrimp and prawns are all on the menu!

Tasmanian devil

On the island of Tasmania, there's a devil living in the forest: the Tasmanian devil. About the size of a bear cub, this marsupial was dubbed a 'devil' because of how it growls and gnarls.

During the daytime, it finds a cosy place between the rocks or in a hollow tree trunk to sleep. But as darkness falls, it forages the forest for food. This little devil is a meat-eater, eating its prey from head to tail: skin, hair, bones, and all. Snakes, birds, fish or chickens, it will eat just about anything it can get its teeth into.

Kangaroo

Many different species of kangaroo, large and small, hop around the Australian plains. And these bouncy marsupials like company: they live in groups of up to 100 kangaroos.

With its large, strong hind legs, the giant kangaroo can jump a distance of more than eight metres. It can be as big as an adult human. Its newborn, however, is only the size of a bean, weighing no more than a feather! A young kangaroo, or a 'joey', lives in its mother's pouch for eight months until it no longer fits. When the joey moves out, its little brother or sister almost immediately takes its place.

Cassowary

This large bird can run fast, jump high and even swim, but it cannot fly. It has a striking appearance with two red wattles on its throat, black feathers on its back, a clear-blue neck and a comb on its head. It uses this comb to push branches and bushes aside in dense forests. Its claws are razor-sharp, and when threatened, the cassowary will use them without hesitation.

Wallaby

Though they are very similar to kangaroos, the wallaby is the smaller of the two. You can also distiguish a wallaby from a kangaroo by its shorter legs: it has less space between its ankle and knee than the kangaroo.

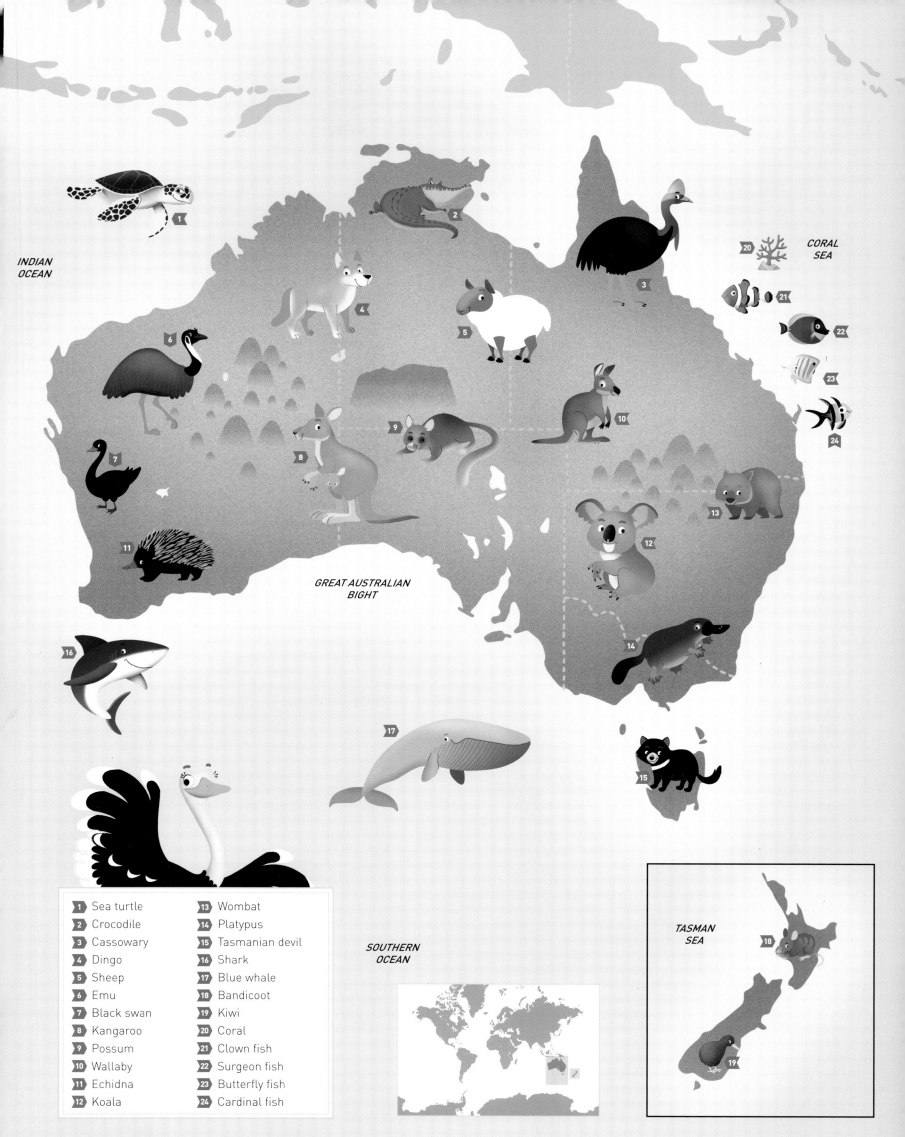

INDIAN
OCEAN

CORAL
SEA

GREAT AUSTRALIAN
BIGHT

SOUTHERN
OCEAN

TASMAN
SEA

1	Sea turtle	13	Wombat
2	Crocodile	14	Platypus
3	Cassowary	15	Tasmanian devil
4	Dingo	16	Shark
5	Sheep	17	Blue whale
6	Emu	18	Bandicoot
7	Black swan	19	Kiwi
8	Kangaroo	20	Coral
9	Possum	21	Clown fish
10	Wallaby	22	Surgeon fish
11	Echidna	23	Butterfly fish
12	Koala	24	Cardinal fish

NORTH POLE

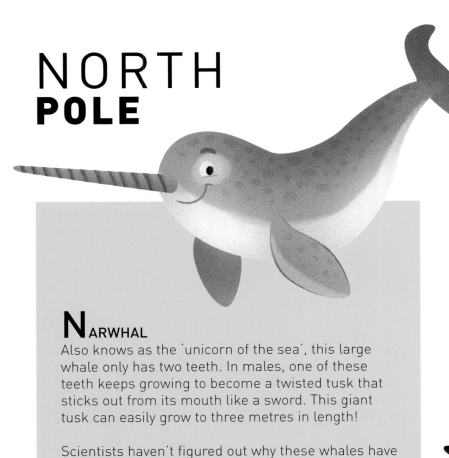

Narwhal

Also knows as the 'unicorn of the sea', this large whale only has two teeth. In males, one of these teeth keeps growing to become a twisted tusk that sticks out from its mouth like a sword. This giant tusk can easily grow to three metres in length!

Scientists haven't figured out why these whales have a tusk. The second tooth usually stays small, but sometimes a narwhal will develop two giant tusks. What a sight that is!

Orca or killer whale

Don't let the name fool you: 'killer whales' are actually the largest of the dolphins. Orcas have a black-and-white patterned skin and a large fin on their backs. On males, this fin can grow to be two metres tall. They are expert hunters and have more than 40 big, sharp teeth in their mouths. These help it crush up fish, penguins, sea lions and even small whales with great ease.

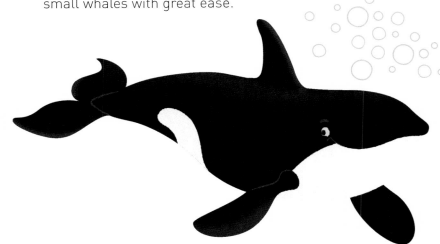

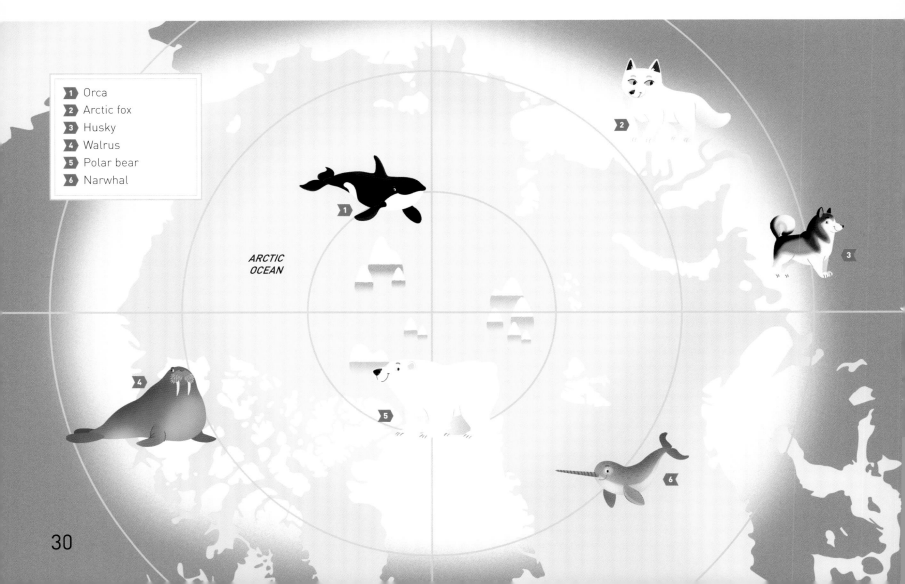

1. Orca
2. Arctic fox
3. Husky
4. Walrus
5. Polar bear
6. Narwhal

ARCTIC OCEAN

Polar bear

The body of this 'King of the North Pole' is perfectly adapted to life in the cold. Its thick coat keeps it warm, even on the ice and its thick layer of fat keeps it warm when swimming in the water. The soles of its paws are hairy, keeping them warm and preventing the bear from slipping on the ice. Its light-coloured fur is perfect camouflage in the icy-white surroundings. This all comes in very handy when you're a dangerous hunter!

Husky

The husky comes from the north of Siberia. It has a thick furry coat to protect it from the cold, snow-covered environment it lives in. It does not like warm weather. This dog is very active and strong. For this reason, it is often used as a sled dog but it is also a great pet.

Arctic fox

The Arctic fox is incredibly resilient. It has adapted well to survive the harsh conditions and the freezing temperatures of the Arctic. Its furry soles allow it to walk on ice. Its thick white coat is the perfect camouflage in the winter, but it darkens and thins out in the summer to allow it to move around unseen between plants and bushes.

This fox lives in a burrow, which is a hole in the ground with many tunnels. This cosy home is often passed down from parents to cubs.

Walrus

This marine animal lives near and in the Arctic ocean. With its long tusks and whiskers, it's a bulky animal that can weight as much as 2,000 kilograms as an adult. That's the same as a small elephant!
Walruses are often found in herds on land. The skin of a young walrus is dark brown, but it grows paler and pink-coloured with age.

A walrus has only three natural enemies: orcas, polar bears and people.

31

SOUTH
POLE

Seal

There are many types of seal, but they can typically be divided into two main groups: seals and true seals. True seals can be distinguished from fur seals, walruses and sea lions by the fact that true seals don't have ears on the outside and can't walk on their hind fins.

Seals can be found in many parts of the world. They spend most of their time in the water, and can stay at sea hunting for weeks. They do have to surface to breathe.

During their breeding time, large groups of seals come to shore where they can easily be spotted and heard. Honking and roaring, these seals make a lot of noise. The groups are mostly females and one male. The strongest males can have up to 40 'wives'. They'll fight off other males who want to take over their group.

Emperor Penguin

The largest of all penguins, the emperors, are well adjusted to the harsh conditions of their ice-cold home. They find safety in numbers and protect themselves from the icy polar winds by huddling up together. Each penguin in the colony will take turns moving from the cold outside to the warm heart of a group, so that no member is on the outside for too long. Emperors actually lay their eggs during the coldest time of the winter. Dad will keep it warm by balancing it on its feet, while Mum goes fishing.

King Penguin

The king penguin is the second largest penguin in the world. It has an orange colour on its cheeks and underneath its chin. The similar, but taller, emperor penguin has a light yellow colour.

Kings breed in enormous groups, sometimes counting up to 100,000 birds. They don't build nests. Like all penguins, the chicks are fed by their parents, with food that Mum and Dad ate the day before. How does this work? The parent vomits the fish it has eaten and the chick eats the fishy paste straight out of its parent's beak. It sounds yucky, but it is the only way to get the food to the little one.

King penguins and emperor penguins may look alike, but their chicks are easy to distinguish. The adult emperor might grow tallest as an adult, its chick is small and grey. The king penguin chick, on the other hand, is much larger and brown.

Rockhopper

The rockhopper can be easily recognised by its 'hairdo' of spiky black and yellow feathers. It also has red eyes and is one of the smallest penguins.

During breeding times, it will dig a burrow to nest in, often using the same one for many years. Both Mum and Dad will take care of the eggs and of the chicks.

This penguin doesn't only live on Antarctica, but also on the shores of Chile and New Zealand.

Gentoo penguin

The Gentoo is the third largest of all penguins. It is easily distinguished from the others by the white stripe on the top of its head and its bright red beak. It also has the longest tail of all penguins. The gentoo colonies prefer to breed on ice-free surfaces where they build a nest with pebbles.

The Gentoo is quite the romantic. The male will 'propose' to his mate with a pebble. When she accepts his proposal, the female will put this pebble in her nest.

Skua bird

The South Pole is often visited by skuas, also known as 'jaegers'. This large predatory gull will mostly eat penguins that are already dead, but given the chance, it will steal an egg or baby penguin too. If it is terribly hungry, it may even attack other birds to steal their dinner. It will grab its competitor's wings until it lets go of its catch.

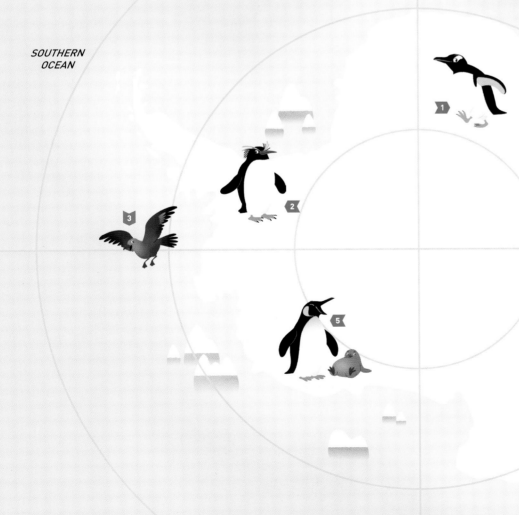

SOUTHERN OCEAN

1 Gentoo penguin
2 Rockhopper
3 Skua bird
4 Seal
5 King penguin
6 Emperor penguin

OCEANS
AND SEAS

BLUE WHALE

The blue whale is the largest known animal to ever live on Earth. It is 30 metres long and can weigh up to 180 tons. Its tongue can even weigh as much as an elephant, its heart the same amount as a car!

This whale might be a giant, but its favourite and maybe only meal is krill: a tiny shrimp-like animal. It will eat tons of krill a day by gulping down a mouthful of water and then forcing the water through its baleen plates. Only the krill is left behind in the whale's mouth, making it easy to swallow.

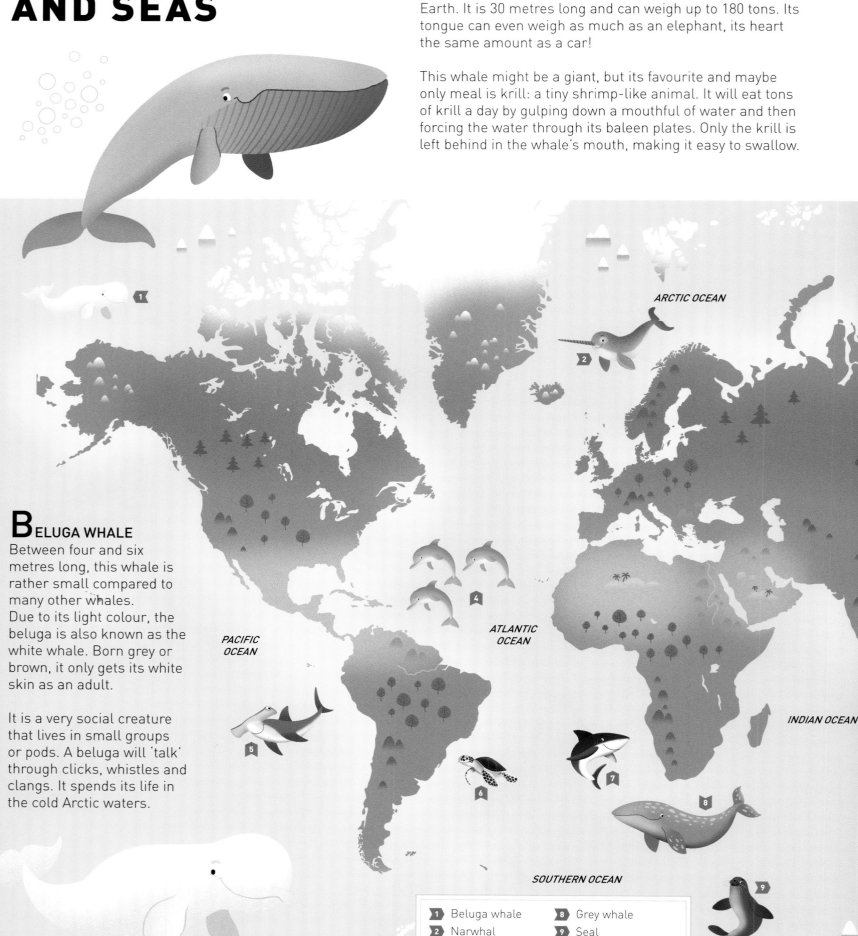

ARCTIC OCEAN

BELUGA WHALE

Between four and six metres long, this whale is rather small compared to many other whales.
Due to its light colour, the beluga is also known as the white whale. Born grey or brown, it only gets its white skin as an adult.

It is a very social creature that lives in small groups or pods. A beluga will 'talk' through clicks, whistles and clangs. It spends its life in the cold Arctic waters.

PACIFIC
OCEAN

ATLANTIC
OCEAN

INDIAN OCEAN

SOUTHERN OCEAN

1	Beluga whale	8	Grey whale
2	Narwhal	9	Seal
3	Bowhead whale	10	Octopus
4	Dolphins	11	Orca
5	Hammerhead shark	12	Clown fish
6	Sea turtle	13	Sailfish
7	Shark	14	Blue whale

Hammerhead Shark

This shark with an unusual head is found in warmer waters worldwide. While it swims in schools of sharks, it does hunt alone. Due to its hammer-shaped head, this shark has a wider view of its surroundings, helping it hunt for food. It can also detect electric fields, allowing it to find stingrays hidden in the sand, helping it avoid being stung.

Clown Fish

This fish is also referred to as an anemone fish, named so after the sea anemones it calls home. It is easily recognised by the three white stripes on its orange skin.

PACIFIC OCEAN

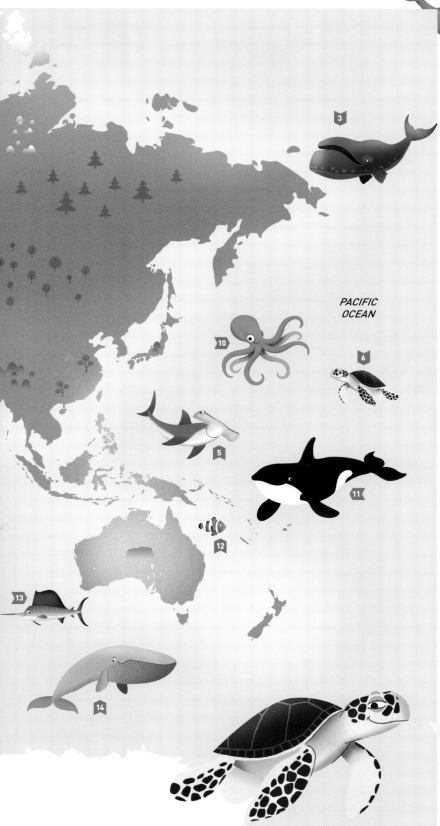

Great Barrier Reef

Off the coast of Australia, in the Coral Sea, lies the largest coral reef in the world. Home to a rich diversity of marine animals, this reef is large enough to be seen from space.

Though coral looks like a plant, it is in fact a structure built by billions of living organisms. Sadly, this giant reef is in danger of going extinct due to pollution and climate change.

EXTINCT
ANIMALS

A species is called 'extinct' when the last of its kind dies and there are no more alive on Earth. Animals can also be 'extinct in the wild' when the only remaining animals of its kind live in zoos. When only a few animals are left alive, the species will be referred to as 'endangered' or 'critically endangered'. Endangered species need extra attention and help in order to survive.

Dutch Alcon Blue Butterfly
This rare butterfly used to call the Netherlands its home. The last one was seen almost 40 years ago.

Madeiran Large White Butterfly
This white butterfly lived in the forests of Madeira. It has not been seen in the last 40 years. It probably went extinct due to a virus infection.

Hawaii 'Ō'ō
This bird, native to the islands of Hawaii, was easily recognised by the yellow feathers on its otherwise black wings and its black-and-white tail. It was hunted for these beautiful feathers. The last bird was seen almost 80 years ago.

PACIFIC
OCEAN

Quagga
This relative of the zebra lived in South Africa until it was hunted into extinction by the Dutch settlers. It had stripes on its head and shoulders and a brown backside.

The last wild quagga died about 150 years ago. The quagga is the first animal to have its DNA mapped in the hopes of one day bringing it back to life.

Golden Toad
This small toad once lived in a small forest region in Costa Rica. The male golden toad was a bright orange colour, while the females could be all colours.

The last golden toad was spotted in 1989. It is thought that it was one of the first species to go extinct due to the consequences of global warming. The golden toad is now seen as a symbol for the endangered status of most amphibians worldwide.

1 Passenger pigeon	**6** Golden toad
2 Hawaii 'Ō'Ō	**7** White rhinoceros
3 Pyrenean ibex	**8** Quagga
4 Dutch alcon blue butterfly	**9** Dodo
5 Madeiran large white butterfly	**10** Tasmanian tiger

ARCTIC OCEAN

ATLANTIC OCEAN

PACIFIC OCEAN

INDIAN OCEAN

SOUTHERN OCEAN

WHITE RHINOCEROS

Don't let its name fool you. The white rhino is actually grey. In fact, the black rhino is grey too! Like all rhinoceroses, the white rhino has a keen sense of hearing and smell. This grass-grazer has a squared lip and two horns on its snout. These horns are the reason for its near extinction: the rhino has been hunted and killed for them.

Although the white rhinoceros is not yet extinct, it is very much endangered. Some other types of rhino have already gone extinct.

DODO

The quirky looking bird can be considered the 'poster bird' for extinct animals. This flightless bird lived on the island of Mauritius. Discovered by Portuguese sailors in the early 16th century, it went extinct less than 200 years later. The dodo was hunted and eaten into extinction by people and by their introduced animals.

37

AMAZING

FAST FOR ITS SIZE

Dragonfly

The biggest dragonflies can fly at about 60 kilometres an hour, crowning them the fastest flying insect. They can fly straight up and down and even hover like a helicopter.

Mantis Shrimp

This rather large shrimp has strong claws that can break glass with a single strike. With a speed of 23 metres per second, its strike is so fast it creates a shockwave which is strong enough to knock its prey or enemy unconscious.

LONG SLEEPER

Lungfish

This eel-like fish has lungs like an amphibian allowing it to breathe in and out of the water. This helps the lungfish during its 'dry sleep'. It will dig itself into a burrow at the bottom of a riverbed or lake bed where it will stay during the dry season when the river or lake dries out. Lungfish can survive in a dry burrow for up to two years.

FAST SWIMMING BIRD

Gentoo Penguin

The gentoo is the third-largest penguin and is recognisable by its red-orange beak.
Though it might walk awkwardly on land, it can swim 36 kilometres an hour, making it the fastest swimmer of all diving birds. But it is the emperor penguin that can dive the deepest.

STRONG BITE

Alligator

The alligator is thought to have the strongest bite of all animals. Its bite is at least 3.5 times stronger than that of other strong biters like hyenas, tigers and lions.

Oddly enough, the jaw muscle that the crocodile needs to open its mouth is rather weak, so its jaw can quite easily be held closed. But of course you shouldn't try this!

FAST

Pronghorn

Though not the fastest runner on the planet, at its top speed of 85 kilometres an hour, the pronghorn does get a silver medal. It might not be able to outrun a cheetah in a sprint, but it will win when running over great distances.

Peregrine Falcon

This bird is found worldwide, with the exception of Antarctica. It soars high in the sky and after spotting its prey, it will dive down to grab its meal at speeds of up to 320 kilometres an hour, making it the fastest animal on Earth!

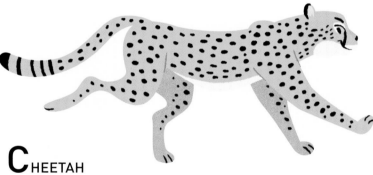

Cheetah

With a top speed of 120 kilometres an hour, the cheetah is the champion when it comes to speed on land. It can speed up from 0 to 100 kilometres an hour in less than three seconds! But it can only run this fast for a short distance.

Sailfish

This fish got its name from the tall and long sail-like fin on its back. It also has a long bill on its snout, much like a swordfish. At 110 kilometres an hour, it's the fastest animal in water.

OLD

Bowhead Whale

It was long believed that bowhead whales could age no older than 100 years. But these water mammals can live twice that long, making them one of the longest living animals on Earth.

Living in the Arctic sea, the bowhead can be recognised by its large head and big lower jaw. And it doesn't have a fin on its back. This whale is completely black with a few white spots on its chin, belly and tail.
The bowhead has a few hundred baleen plates in its mouth to allow it to feed on plankton. Its baleen plates are the biggest of all whales.

Giant Tortoise

Giant tortoises can become much older than people, easily more than 150 years old.
Another remarkable thing is that this 'giant' can go without food for a very long time, sometimes even more than a year.

AMAZING
JUMPER

Red KANGAROO
The largest of all marsupials is a fast hopper thanks to its powerful hind legs. It can hop at a speed of 55 kilometres an hour. In a single leap it can jump a whopping distance of eight metres, or reach a height of two metres. That's higher than any other animal!

Snow LEOPARD
This grey leopard isn't just pretty, it's also the best jumper in the animal kingdom! It can cover 15 metres in one leap, using its long tail to balance it. This means it would be able to jump over a school bus.

Grasshopper
A grashopper is a supreme jumper given its size. In a single bound, it can travel distances 20 times its own length and reach heights that are 10 times its own length. Amazing!

UNIQUE

Hummingbird
This small bird has many amazing traits. It can beat its wings faster than any other bird, can hover in air, and it is the only bird that can fly backwards!
Being one of the smallest birds in the world, it also lays the smallest eggs of all birds.

Blue DRAGON
This beautiful sea creature is actually a type of slug. You wouldn't guess it because it looks spectacular, but it is in fact camouflaged. While its blue side blends in with the blue of the water, its grey side can hardly be distinguished from the sea's surface.

Don't let its looks fool you, this pretty critter is venomous. It can even absorb the poison of its prey, to use later during its next hunt.

Phasmatodea
Stick insects and leaf insects are types of phasmatodea. They are masters of camouflage. They look just like the plant they call home, making it difficult to be spotted by attackers. So a stick insect looks like a twig or branch and a leaf insect looks like... a leaf!

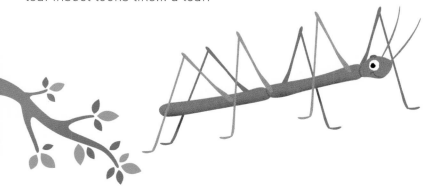